RENEW YOUR MIND, MAXIMIZE YOUR POTENTIAL

RUTH VERBREE

REEVERB
Publishing

Publisher:

ReeVerb Publishing

Kamloops, BC

Canada

Printed in Canada and the United States

CONTENTS

Ruth is an aspiring business woman whose desire is to help people become mentally fit by empowering them through her own experiences and insight. Staying positive is a key component in staying mentally healthy. In her journey through 35 years with a spouse in law enforcement, she has witnessed first-hand the many challenges and victories that happen in life. She saw the need to stay positive in a negative world.

She cared for her husband and stayed by his side as he hit rock bottom with mental illness. She helped her husband turn the corner and climb back up to the light. It is her desire now to create awareness, and help break the negative stigma that still surrounds mental illness.

#Turnthelighton

Ruth wants you to know that there is hope for the future. You can Renew Your Mind and Maximize Your Potential. You can become mentally fit and live your dream life.

Ruth currently resides in Kamloops, British Columbia, Canada, with her husband, retired RCMP (Royal Canadian Mounted Police) officer of 35 years, and lives near her children and grandchildren. She is now working together with a team of professionals building an online platform to help educate, to create awareness, and to engage and empower you to become the best you can be.

Renew Your Mind, Maximize Your Potential

INTRODUCTION

Renew Your Mind, Maximize Your Potential is all about how to transform your life, and change your outlook so that you can unlock your full potential to achieve success.

My life has been full of adventures, some extraordinary and some not so grandiose, yet they are still my life's adventures. The same is true for you, only your stories are somewhat different from mine. There is one thing in common though, you and I have both had our ups and downs. Each and every person has good and bad days, yet it seems as though most people focus on the bad days rather than the good ones.

It seems easier for people to hang onto or recall bad memories than to enjoy and linger on the wonderful memories they hold dear to their hearts. With this book, it is my hope and desire that my simple - but not always easy - strategies will help you begin to have more positive days ahead, and that by following these recommendations, your life will improve in some tangible ways.

Through a unique series of experiences, I have cracked the code on maximizing my human potential - I want to share that code with you!

You have one life to live, so cheers to you for reading this book and implementing these strategies. Watch as your days get a little bit brighter.

CHAPTER ONE

INTROSPECTION

IN EACH CHAPTER, we have an *Introspection* section. To get the most out of those sections of this book, I would suggest having a pen handy. If you are the type of person who loves to journal or keep a logbook of some sort, this is where you should begin writing down the next steps. However, we will include some space to write down some thoughts as well. Take a moment to think through the Introspection questions before moving onto the next one. Write down the thoughts coming through your head, and put them on paper so that you can look back later and see the progress you have made.

I want to let you know how important renewing your mind and maximizing your potential is to your mental health and what that really means.

Firstly, what is mental health?

Mental health is "a state of well-being in which the individual realizes his or her own abilities, can cope with the normal stresses of life, can work productively and fruitfully, and is able to make a contribution to his or her community."

Take a moment to consider your own mental health.

Do you believe you are mentally healthy? (Remember that mentally healthy doesn't mean problem free, it means you are in the right headspace to take on the day's challenges).

Can you cope with the stress of your current day-to-day life? What are the biggest contributors of your day-to-day stress? Spend some time thinking about everything involved in your life. This might include certain responsibilities at your job (or business), your family, your coworkers or business partners, finances, the physical health of yourself or someone close to you, your unreliable vehicle situation; it could be anything.

Feel free to write some of these down. Spend a moment pondering each item on your list that causes you stress. Think about whether or not these are things that you can control. Sometimes when you realize that you cannot control everything going on around you, it helps you let go of the hold it has on you. Worrying about what goes on around you when you can't change it, is wasted effort. If you still can't let go of it, think about it from another perspective. Think to yourself, "In five years, will this matter?" Even if it's only one year, most of the things you are stressing about will tend not to matter in a year from now, let alone five years from now.

One theory developed by Dr. Carol Ryff, the Hilldale Professor of Psychology at the University of Wisconsin-Madison, suggests six factors which contribute to an individual's well-being, contentment and happiness. She states that "mental health consists of positive relationships with others, personal mastery, autonomy, a feeling of purpose and meaning in life, and personal growth and development. Psychological well-being is attained by achieving a state of balance affected by both challenging and rewarding life events."

So let's look at those six factors that contribute to an individual's well-being, contentment, and happiness.

It is significant to note that Professor Ryff's explanation begins with positive relationships with others. Having positive connections with family, friends, and acquaintances, and having a connection with a broader community is of primary importance.

Personal mastery is a journey. It is pursued, not achieved. Think of personal mastery in your job or business. It's never perfect, but it can continually be improved as it approaches perfection. Sometimes personal mastery can be enjoyable, but other times the things that need to change in your life are difficult. The most difficult things to change can also be the most rewarding.

Autonomy is the freedom from external control or the ability to control one's own actions. This external control may exist in any part of your life, from a significant other (spouse), to a parent, child, business partner or overbearing friend.

A feeling of purpose and meaning. This would be the reason why you are doing what you are doing and what that looks like when you've accomplished it. Do you know why you've chosen this path that you are on? People that have their purpose figured out are able to persevere through great amounts of stress knowing what their end goal is.

Personal growth is the development and understanding of your own self to achieve your full potential. For you, this will look different than the person next to you. You have a different personality so your journey will look different. Typically, but not always, personal development consists of taking personality traits that are often looked at in a negative aspect and using them to further your success. Stubbornness, for example, is a common one. However, with the right amount and when applied appropriately, stubbornness can be seen as tenacity. Often your most powerful, positive traits can be taken too far and become negative. True wisdom is learning this balance.

Dr. Jeanne Segal, another psychologist who has done a great deal of work in the field of optimal mental health, suggests that people who are mentally healthy have the following eight characteristics:

- A sense of contentment.
- A zest for living and the ability to laugh and have fun.
- The ability to deal with stress and bounce back from adversity.
- A sense of meaning and purpose, in both their activities and their relationships.
- The flexibility to learn new things and adapt to change.
- A balance between work and play, rest and activity, etc.
- The ability to build and maintain fulfilling relationships.
- Self-confidence and high self-esteem.

Take another moment and check yourself on each one of these points. These positive characteristics of mental and emotional health allow you to participate in life to the fullest extent possible through productive, meaningful activities and strong relationships. These positive characteristics also help you cope when faced with life's challenges and stresses.

You may not have everything in perfect proportions. For example, your work/life balance may be way off to one side because this week you are going away on business for a week. Make sure to take some time the week before or after to spend time on the things you enjoy or with the people that are important in your life to maintain this balance.

As you go through this book, make sure that you take the time to work through each of the introspection sections. This will give you a clear sense of where you are at, and it will give you a sense of how you can improve. It's all part of the journey to Maximize Your Potential!

CHAPTER TWO

ENVISIONING A POSITIVE DAY

Before getting out of bed, envision a positive day.

YOUR ALARM GOES off and startles you out of a deep sleep. It's far too early. You roll over and reach for the snooze button. You desperately want to snooze, but know you shouldn't. It's too late; you've already hit the button and now you have 10 more minutes to drift away. But before you drift back off, a different alarm starts to ring in your head. You vaguely recall you made the decision late last night not to drift away again, but to take the minutes you normally snooze to envision what your day is going to look like. You rub your eyes, and attempt to awaken your mind and try to conjure up images for what your positive day will be.

Your mind is fuzzy. All you can think of is that you need to have a shower, make coffee, and you have to be at work by 8:00 am. You have a number of emails to reply to before 9:00 am, a team meeting after that, and then a lunch appointment with a coworker. The afternoon is unknown at this point.

Here is one way to envision your day. Begin by envisioning your whole day progressing smoothly and positively.

I want to sleep, but instead I see myself placing my feet onto the comfy, warm rug beside my bed, stepping into my cozy slippers and walking to the kitchen. I envision turning on the subdued lighting and getting my coffee brewing. I try and imagine the aroma - oh how I love the smell of my morning coffee. The scent drifts into my mind and I inwardly smile, anticipating my morning brew. I have a smile on my face now, and my positive day has begun. As my coffee is brewing, I see myself stepping into the shower, feeling the hot water streaming over my entire face and body, enjoying its warmth along with the faint scent of my floral body wash - I inwardly feel fresh and new.

I see myself drying off with my large, soft bath towel, and then scrambling to get dressed before the cold brings me back to reality. I love the warmth of the shower, like the rays of the sun penetrating my skin. Dressed, I return to the kitchen and pour myself a large cup of coffee, inhaling its rich aroma and lingering on the first sip, enjoying the sensation it gives me.

I want to stay calm and relaxed, so I plan to give myself enough time to get to work, allowing time to listen to my favourite song and avoiding the rush of traffic and the frenzy of frantic drivers. I work through the rest of my routine, gathering my lunch from the fridge, and I'm out the door in plenty of time. I even have enough time to pour myself another coffee to enjoy on the drive to work. I arrive at work 10 minutes early, so I am not rushed and panicking about all the emails I need to get through. I stop and say hi to my coworker, but I don't chat as long as usual so that I don't get behind on my to-do list.

My day is going well. I now envision that I have completed all my tasks and am early for my morning meeting. All is well. I am prepared and the morning has gone the way I envisioned it.

Next I see myself going to my lunch appointment. Ahhh yes, what to eat? I will enjoy a healthy meal, and make healthy choices for myself. My coworker and I enjoy our conversation together. The afternoon goes well and my day has been pleasant and productive.

Now I envision the drive home at the end of the day. I have accomplished a lot at work and I feel good about myself. As I drive home, I contemplate what to make for dinner. Yes, I can see what I am making and I have all the ingredients at home. I am prepared. I have made another good choice on healthy eating. I have stayed on track and am positive.

I would like to take a walk after dinner, so I envision where I will walk, and in my mind I can see the little path that leads up to the trail and onto the meadow. I love this nature trail, so I look forward to this time after work where I can get outside and get close to nature. There are still a few more tasks I need to accomplish before I can read my book, so I envision doing those tasks after I get in from my exercise time out in nature. I feel good about myself - I have completed my checklist and I can now sit and relax and read my book or just watch TV. How wonderful! I love to curl up on the couch and have some downtime. Hmmmm, I think to myself, it's been an awesome day, a very positive day.

The snooze button sounds and you jolt upright. You just saw your whole day in front of you and you are amazed at how good it was. You are invigorated and now you want to get up and carry out your plan as you just envisioned it. You are looking forward to a very positive day today.

MAXIMIZE YOUR POTENTIAL

Think about the day ahead of you. As you contemplate what the day will hold, it is important to visualize the events through a positive lens. Here is a scenario on how you could maximize your potential by envisioning a positive day.

You are heading into a facilitated one-day, 8-hour course and you know that there is going to be a test at the end of the day.

You suffer from test anxiety, and know that you have to exercise your mental fitness to maximize your potential for this day.

You decide to wake up 20 minutes early, because you want to spend extra time envisioning yourself mastering the test calmly. In your mind, you begin writing the exam, calmly and positively.

This 8-hour course is important to you because it will enable you to perform better, and passing the exam will help you obtain certain promotions in the future. This will soon equate to more dollars in your pocket. You will also receive a certificate to prove it! You can already taste the success because you are visualizing it. You are maximizing your potential through positivity.

You begin envisioning other aspects of your positive day . You see yourself walking into the meeting room; you see tables and chairs set up throughout the room. Where will you sit? You choose a place in the second row, so you can see the white board and the facilitator easily.

You see your workbook, and your name tag. You envision working through the chapters, taking notes throughout the pages, and working on name associations to remember the information so that you will be ready to answer the questions on the test. Everything is going according to plan.

It's lunchtime, and you see yourself taking a quick break to go stretch your legs and take a quick walk. You go pick up a healthy lunch and a coffee and sit back and close your eyes to rest your mind for a few minutes. Then your enjoy your healthy lunch and head back into class.

The afternoon flies by. You feel the tension rising in your back and neck and consciously take some deep long breaths. The deep breathing helps you feel calmer. You know you can do it.

The last hour has now arrived. The test papers are handed out.

You smile inwardly and see yourself carefully writing your name on the paper. Your hands and fingers are calm. You take another deep breath and tell yourself "I've got this!" You feel calm and collected and are ready to maximize your potential.

Envision the positive. Plan to master the outcome.

CHAPTER 2 INTROSPECTION

INTROSPECTION

How does this story apply to you? Dedicate some time before you start your day to think about what is coming your way. What is your current morning routine? Is it positive, negative or neutral?

_____

_____

_____

_____

_____

Are you a daydreamer or dreader? Is there a situation, a conversation, or something controversial you need to deal with that could go either way? Walk yourself through every step of the scenario. For example, if you have to confront a coworker about something they said, and you are expecting them to be defensive, will that expectation come out in how you communicate with them? Instead, if you are expecting that what you say will be well received, you are more likely to communicate in a positive way.

_____

_____

_____

_____

_____

When you have been expecting positive things to happen, you will have built up your self-confidence to handle whatever it is you need to handle.

When you have seen the positive outcome in your mind, it is far more likely to turn out the way you envisioned it because your confidence shows up with you. Even when it doesn't turn out like you envisioned, your ability to see the positive will help you respond more appropriately which will create a better outcome!

Do you believe that your attitude can alter the course of the day?

> *Two guys are driving down the highway when the truck they are in runs over a nail and they get a flat tire.*

> *They pull over and get out to inspect. One of the guys is cursing up a storm about their misfortune. The other is whistling a happy tune and smiling.*

> *The grumpy guy turns to the happy one and asks, "Why on earth are you happy about this?"*

The happy guy replies, "this is number 16."

*"16 what?" The grumpy guy responds, "You've had
16 flats?"*

*"That's exactly how many flats I've had." The happy
guy said. "In a lifetime, the average person gets 18
flat tires. That means I've only got two left!"*

How do you think that the rest of their day carried on after
having a flat tire? How you respond to a situation can significantly impact the direction your day goes. If you constantly
make the same choice, your life will reflect that same choice.

_____

_____

_____

_____

_____

* * *

**Dream and give yourself permission to envision a You
that you choose to be.**

-Joy Page

CHAPTER THREE

THE IMPORTANCE OF DAILY MEDITATION

Listening to meditations on a daily basis is beneficial for staying positive.

YOU MAY SCOFF at the words: meditation, relaxation, power of the mind, healing mindfulness etc. Some will recognize the importance of these words, and how these words can bring light to your soul and have a positive influence in your life. Meditations can realign your mind with your body; they can change your paradigm and help to alter your subconscious mind. You need to filter out the negative stuff if your goal is to be positive, and listening to meditations regularly can certainly help renew your mind.

Meditation means different things to different people. It can mean reading an inspirational poem and dwelling on the words for a time; it can mean reading your Bible or reading some other thought provoking message, or it can mean praying to your Creator or reciting creeds. For some it can mean journaling and baring their souls to pen and paper. It can mean doing pilates or yoga, going for a walk, doing a relaxation exercise which involves deep breathing that takes your mind to a safe place, or it can mean listening to music that brings you closer to your Maker and allows you to worship.

The important thing to remember about meditation is that you are trying to achieve mental and emotional clarity. You want to be present and be in the moment.

What time of day is best for you? You need to be in a safe and comfortable environment where you can focus on the task at hand, a place where you can listen to your meditations uninter-rupted. You need to be relaxed and in a space where you can appreciate this quiet time and give your full attention to your meditations or your prayerful worship times. For many people, getting up 10 to 30 minutes earlier is a way to fit this into their day. For other people, it is before they go to bed, when the day is done and the lights are out and they can finally totally relax. Still other people can take 10 minutes here and there, maybe after lunch before they go to work in the afternoon, or maybe while they are commuting to work and back. You just need to figure out what time works best for you and then implement it until it becomes a habit. This habit will soon become part of your daily routine that you anticipate and will help make everyday a little more positive.

Meditations are a great tool to add to your tool-belt and can be used almost anywhere. You can "plug-in" while you grocery shop and listen to something that helps keep you calm. You can multitask in the kitchen rather than watching something nega-tive and depressing on the television. Why not listen to an inspi-rational story or something that lifts you up and puts positive ideas in your head versus the negative that is so often prevalent in the News?

Meditations are wonderful when you listen to them regularly.

They start to change your self image and change your subconscious mind. You begin to have more hope and faith and are able to relax easier as you learn the breathing techniques that many meditations provide. They can motivate you and help you gain a new perspective on life.

Soon you will look forward to your time of meditation each day and it will become routine or habit without even knowing it. This positive influence in your life will be a game changer that will help you renew your mind and maximize your potential. What you feed into your mind, comes out in your heart.

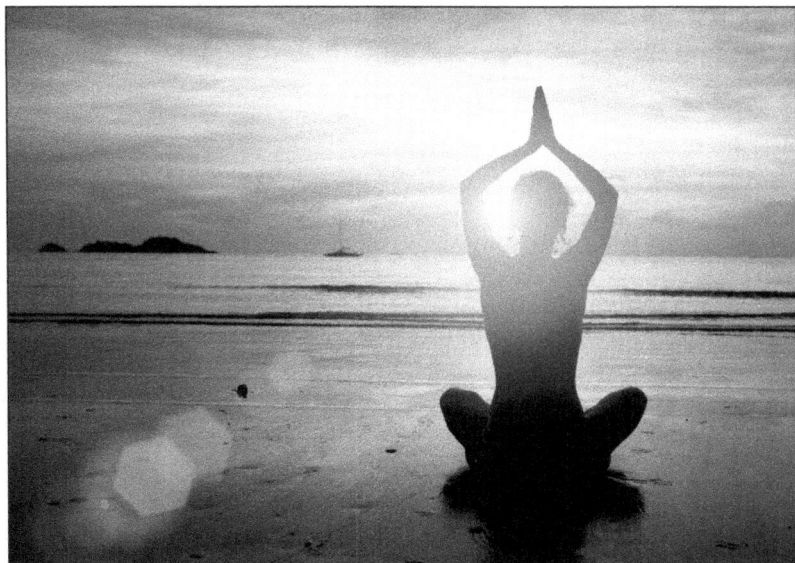

We know there are so many benefits of meditation or mindfulness, but here is a list of 8 Ways Meditation Can Improve Your Life from Kristine Crane at the Huffington Post.

1. Meditation reduces stress.

2. Meditation improves concentration.

3. Meditation encourages a healthy lifestyle.

4. Meditation increases self-awareness.

5. Meditation increases happiness.

6. Meditation increases acceptance.

7. Meditation slows aging.

8. Meditation benefits cardiovascular and immune health.

So with these eight benefits in mind, you have a lot to gain by following a routine of daily meditation. In order to help empower yourself and improve your life, I would encourage you to take up the habit. Try it for yourself and see how it helps you experience a more positive day!

MAXIMIZE YOUR POTENTIAL

How will you maximize your potential through daily meditation?

Meditation might be uncomfortable to you if you have not done this before, but be rest assured that through daily meditation, your body will thank you once you have gotten into the habit.

Maximizing your potential through meditation means taking the time to focus on what is important to you. For example, you might use meditation to empower yourself to increase your wealth. Perhaps you are using meditation to increase your physical, spiritual, social or emotional health. Decide what you want to gain out of meditation and then think of ways that meditation will maximize your potential. There are many different meditations to engage in and you will want to find out what style and technique works for you.

Here is one scenario that works to maximize your potential through meditation in the work world.

If you are an employee or own a business, it is important to have a mind that can focus on the here and now. It is important to practice being still, calm, and collected, because during an interview or a presentation, or when meeting a new client, you will want to present yourself as someone who is collected, attentive, has clarity, and can focus on the task at hand.

Meditation can help you stay calm. When you get into the habit, you can meditate anywhere from 10 to 60 minutes at a time, and this daily practice will help your body learn how to stay calm and focused for long periods of time. This may be just what saves you in your future interview or presentation. This will definitely maximize your potential!

Meditation, when done habitually, also has some excellent health benefits, seen in the list above. You will reap the health benefits in the long term, not just the short term. You might want to consider doing meditation strictly for the long term health benefits, because your health is vital for you to love and live out your dream life.

If you are losing sleep because of too much stress, meditation will help reduce your stress, which in turn will help you sleep. Getting more sleep will make you feel more mentally alert, which will then help you be more productive throughout each day. Find out what works for you and reap the benefits of putting in the effort.

Meditation is an exercise for mental fitness that you will want to practice - it will help you maximize your potential.

CHAPTER 3 INTROSPECTION

INTROSPECTION

Do you currently meditate? What does that look like? If not, what holds you back from trying it?

_____

_____

_____

_____

_____

If you try meditation and you find that its not working for you, feel free to try different methods or different times of the day to get a different experience. Some people meditate through exercise such as yoga, while others meditate through reading scriptures, and still others meditate by being part of nature - there is no right or wrong way. You just have to find what works for you!

Journal your thoughts. Write down the benefits that you have experienced from meditation or if you haven't started yet, think about the benefits that you want to get from meditation.

_____

_____

_____

_____

_____

_____

_____

_____

_____

_____

After meditating, did you see how it helped you live in the present? How do you think this has helped you maximize your potential? What benefits do you see from what you experienced? Why is this important?

_____

_____

_____

_____

_____

* * *

The purpose of meditation is to make our mind calm and peaceful. If our mind is peaceful, we will be free from worries and mental discomfort, and so we will experience true happiness. But if our mind is not peaceful, we will find it very difficult to be happy, even if we are living in the very best conditions.

-Kelsang Gyatso

CHAPTER FOUR

AWAKENING IN NATURE

Taking a walk in nature is more than just exercise.

THERE ARE SO many benefits to walking. Not only is it good exercise, which helps build your strength, tones muscle and develops perseverance, but walking is also recommended for cardiovascular and overall physical health. It is also recommended for mental health. Walking can help you clear your mind and it lets you work through decisions that you need to make. You can walk before work, after work, or in spurts throughout your day. You can walk for fun, walk for physical exercise, walk to de-stress, walk with a purpose or chat with a friend, or you can take a leisurely walk out in nature, which has even more added benefits to help make your day more positive.

Getting up early and walking in the crisp morning air can awaken your senses and you can enjoy the sunrise as you begin setting the stage for a positive day. You can enjoy the quiet of the early morning and the stillness of life, listening to the sounds of nature as the world comes alive. You will learn to hear and appreciate the birds singing, the wind rustling the leaves, crickets chirping and frogs croaking. You will become more aware of your surroundings and the little things in life will start to take on new meaning. When you "stop and smell the roses" so to speak, your day becomes a little more beautiful and calm.

You can also listen to a variety of podcasts, music or motivational speakers while you walk, which will also help set the stage for a positive day. These talks are inspiring and invigorating and can help you accomplish more by motivating you to move forward in your life. There is audio self-help available, you just have to find what works for you and begin to incorporate it into your daily life. While you walk, you can get in touch with your inner self, work through things that you might otherwise not have the time for and come away feeling refreshed, like a brand new person. Even daydreaming of your next vacation while you walk can lighten the load and allow your thoughts to relax and calm your body.

Going for a walk at sunset is another beautiful time of day where you can reflect and celebrate the positive day you have had and for what you have accomplished throughout your day. This can give you the feeling of satisfaction and a sense of contentment that makes for a beautiful, peaceful evening.

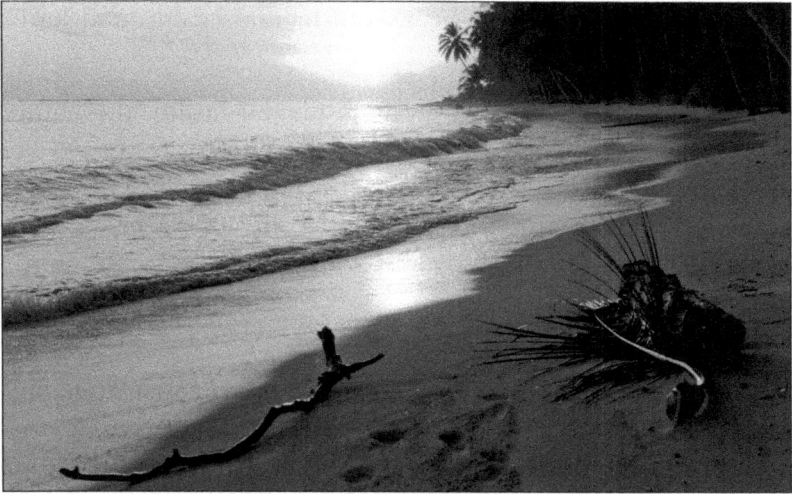

According to the Mayo Clinic, walking has many benefits and here are just a few from their site.

1. Walking helps to maintain a healthy weight.
2. Walking prevents or manages various conditions, including heart disease, high blood pressure and type 2 diabetes.
3. Walking helps strengthen your bones and muscles.
4. Walking improves your mood.
5. Walking improves your balance and coordination.

With all these health benefits alone, walking is extremely valuable, but then adding nature to the walk, you are sure to glean added positivity to your day.

"The study, conducted by researchers at the University of Michigan, found that taking group nature walks is associated with a whole host of mental health benefits, including decreased depression, improved well-being and mental health, and lower perceived stress."

"In addition to seeming to promote mental health, the nature group walks also 'appear to mitigate the effects of stressful life events on perceived stress and negative affect while synergizing with physical activity to improve positive affect and mental well-being,' according to the study abstract."

According to Sara Warber (associate profession of family medicine at the U-M Medical School, "Walking is an inexpensive, low risk and accessible form of exercise and it turns out that combined with nature and group settings, it may be a very powerful, under-utilized stress buster." She also stated that, "Our findings suggest that something as simple as joining an outdoor walking group may not only improve someone's daily positive emotions but may also contribute a non-pharmacological approach to serious conditions like depression."

With all of this in mind, it is very clear that a walk out in nature is sure to enhance your day in a positive way and therefore will maximize your potential.

MAXIMIZE YOUR POTENTIAL

Walking is one of the keys to unlocking the potential for your dream life. Walking has so many great benefits that you will want to make it a priority in your life.

Aside from all the health benefits walking has, it takes you away from distractions and gives you time to think and work through issues. It can also get your creative juices flowing and be the catalyst that will help you plan and work out the details of things going on in your life.

Giving yourself the pleasure of walking in nature helps to boost your mood, and when your mood is up, your potential sky rockets. You then have the confidence needed to tackle whatever comes your way.

Getting out in nature also helps to ground you and helps you untangle your thoughts. It brings you down to earth, and gives you time to connect with your Creator, your Maker, your Higher Power. This may be a time when you allow your mind to wander deep into your soul and you maximize your spiritual potential. The Bible says "Seek, and you will find." You might search for your "why" and find your true purpose. Renewing your mind and searching your heart will bring you to a place where you are at peace with yourself. Feeling at peace with yourself will help you move forward as the best version of yourself.

Walking and talking can maximize your potential in your relationships as well. While you walk and talk, learning to work through hard issues can help you maximize your potential. While you walk, your words are projected out in front of you rather than directed face to face, and sometimes this makes it easier to communicate and say the hard things that lovingly need to be said. The words might be the same words, but somehow when they are not spoken directly face to face, you have the strength to speak them.

One last suggestion on how to maximize your potential is to talk through your goals and dreams while you walk, either with your partner or a trusted friend. Your creative juices will help you figure out the solutions to your problems, and will help you to achieve your goals. In this way, you are renewing your mind and maximizing your potential.

CHAPTER 4 INTROSPECTION

INTROSPECTION

Spend some time in nature, whether it's going for a walk in a park or on the beach but be surrounded by nature and nothing else. Close your eyes and reach out with your other senses.

Describe what you feel. Think of all of your senses and pause for a moment to focus on each one.

_____

_____

_____

_____

_____

Can you taste anything in the air? Is it the salt from the ocean?

_____

_____

What can you smell? Is it the humid air of the forest?

_____

_____

_____

What do you feel? Is it the sand under your feet? Or is it the rough bark on a tree?

_____

_____

_____

What do you see? Do you see an orchestra of color displayed in a rainbow?

_____

_____

_____

Can you hear nature? Are there animals or is it the wind rustling through the trees?

_____

_____

_____

Do you recharge in nature? Can you feel an improvement of your disposition or mental state after being outside in nature?

_____

_____

_____

Write down what you experienced and how taking that time to experience nature helped add positivity to your day.

_____

_____

_____

_____

_____

_____

_____

_____

_____

* * *

Look deep into nature, and then you will understand everything better.

-Albert Einstein

CHAPTER FIVE

ENJOY DAYDREAMING

A dose of daydreaming helps the mind relax.

WHEN WAS the last time you allowed yourself time to sit and daydream? When was the last time you let your mind wander to a faraway place where happily ever after made you smile? I remember my parents telling me to stop daydreaming and finish my task at hand. Yet for you who still daydream, you might find comfort and solace in allowing yourself time to go beyond to that faraway land. This can be very healthy and can start your creative juices flowing freely.

Wikipedia says "daydreaming is a short-term detachment from one's immediate surroundings, during which a person's contact with reality is blurred and partially substituted by a visionary fantasy, especially one of happy, pleasant thoughts, hopes or ambitions, imagined as coming to pass, and experienced while awake."

Notice that the emphasis is on pleasant, happy thoughts and

hopes and ambitions coming to pass. This is very intriguing, as the saying goes - you become what you think about.

Daydreaming can influence you positively and here is a list of its benefits.

1. People who daydream are more likely to have empathy.
2. Daydreaming can lower blood pressure.
3. Mind wandering promotes creativity.
4. Daydreaming, like nighttime dreaming, consolidates learning.
5. A wandering mind usually has a better working memory.

"In a University of California at Santa Barbara study, students who were given an extremely boring task, meant to elicit mind-wandering, were better able to come up with ideas for unusual ways to use items. That means when you're given the opportunity to daydream, your unconscious mind can think of creative solutions to problems."

So daydreaming isn't a bad thing, in fact, it's a very positive thing. Here is an example of what daydreaming may look like as you begin to allow yourself time for creative mind boosting for your positive day.

> *I take in a few deep breaths, feeling the air flowing in through my nose and out through my mouth. As I feel the breath flowing into my chest and heart, my mind goes beyond the clouds, and the colour of the sky wraps around my body and makes me dream of the ocean, the vivid colours of the water. I see myself floating along, being carried away to the warm place where I will never grow old. I enjoy the rocking of the waves and I begin to drift away, closing my eyes to what was and opening my eyes to what is - my secret*

place, where I am loved by all those around me. I am now on a beautiful island, where the the white sand curls around my toes and the turquoise water engulfs my body and my heart to overflowing. I am in love with nature, in love with those who inhabit the island, those who surround me, and they love me unconditionally in return. The island is a world where there is only peace and freedom. I am calm and relaxed and full of gratitude. There is light that illuminates each soul and creates an atmosphere of pure joy. My heart is ready to explode and I take another deep breath that brings me back to reality.

You shake your head and wonder if you had dozed off and were really dreaming or whether your mind actually daydreamed so vividly.

Create your own daydream. Imagination comes easier the more you do it, so just let your mind begin to conjure up beautiful images or places that will serve as a positive memory for you to take into your day. These daydreams can help you focus on staying positive, so give yourself the opportunity and relax your mind. Renew your mind, and this will maximize your potential.

MAXIMIZE YOUR POTENTIAL

How does daydreaming maximize your potential?

You may think that daydreaming is childish, but in order for you to maximize your potential, daydreaming is a definite skill to add to your toolbelt. There is an incredible power that comes from the subconscious mind, and this power happens to come through the act of daydreaming. How awesome is that!!!

So put away the negative thoughts that hinder you from daydreaming and let your super-intelligence get to work for you. Your subconscious mind uses daydreaming, feelings, and images to guide you and bring out your genius.

Here is a scenario that will resonate with you on how daydreaming will maximize your potential. Change the action to represent what you see yourself doing. If your goal is to design a website, then daydream about your website. If your goal is to write a book, then see your name on the cover of the book. Here is a daydream about public speaking.

Through a unique series of experiences you went through, you wanted to become a public speaker and share your story.

You started this journey by first getting rid of the limiting beliefs you had about speaking. Then you began to daydream and see yourself holding a microphone. You saw the people in the room. At first, there were just a few people in the audience, but as your imagination improved, your daydreaming took you to bigger crowds. You saw the spotlights shining on yourself, and you saw yourself shaking from nerves before you began to speak. You felt the butterflies in your stomach. You saw yourself begin to emerge and break free from the fear.

Next you daydreamed about being asked to come and speak. Organizations were contacting you, and now your audiences were even bigger. They were coming to hear you speak! Your story was impacting other lives and you were living your dream.

Your daydreaming took you international. You were getting bigger and your name was getting out there. People started to talk about your story and wanted to come and see you in person. You came alive and the stage was an adrenaline rush and you wanted more.

Soon you were sharing the stage with the big leagues. You were on stage with motivational speakers and world renowned names like Les Brown, Raymond Aaron, and James MacNeil. You had made it. You saw the crowd applaud you and could feel the energy in the room. It was your time to shine!

Your daydreaming went farther. You saw the texts and the emails, the comments that said you had helped people make the right decision. You had given someone else hope to carry on. You had made a difference in this person's life, and they were sharing your story to pass this hope to someone else.

Daydreaming about speaking becomes your reality. Daydreaming makes it come alive. Daydreaming will maximize your potential too!

CHAPTER 5 INTROSPECTION

INTROSPECTION

Are you a daydreamer? Can you see the positive benefits of daydreaming?

_____

_____

_____

Have you ever experienced the creative surge during or after daydreaming? What did it feel like?

_____

_____

_____

What do you daydream about? What does your life look like while you daydream? What is different about your life when you daydream, compared to your real life?

_____

_____

_____

_____

_____

Journal your thoughts about what you experienced.

_____

_____

_____

_____

_____

_____

_____

_____

_____

* * *

That daydreaming mode turns out to be restorative. It's like hitting the reset button in your brain. And you don't get in that daydreaming mode typically by texting and Facebooking. You get in it by disengaging.

-Daniel Levitin

CHAPTER SIX

STATE YOUR INTENTION DAILY

An intention a day, keeps negativity at bay!

WHAT DO you think about when you hear the word intention? Do you have a positive immediate response or do you immediately react and turn to the stressors of work? The word intention defined in the dictionary means a thing intended, an aim or plan. At dictionary.com, "intent is chiefly legal or literary: attack with intent to kill. Purpose implies having a goal or determination to achieve something." Some of you would, therefore, immediately dwell on your work or think of a legal response.

The Cambridge dictionary, however, implies that intention is something that you want and plan to do. The Merriam-Webster dictionary says intention is the thing that you plan to do or achieve: an aim or a purpose.

So let's see how this looks then when you want to state your intention, daily. I am referring to this as your purpose for a positive daily outlook on life. You want to speak your intention so that you are reinforcing to yourself that you aim to have a positive day. You plan to achieve positivity in your life daily, and by speaking this intention into your life everyday, you are intending it to come true. Sometimes your mind tells you the opposite of what you are stating, and you begin to doubt what you are speaking. Your subconscious mind can feed you with negative thoughts and doubts and you need to conquer these feelings that make you doubt yourself. You need to change your subconscious mind in order for you to live out your intentions, and speaking positive intentions everyday will help you renew your mind for positivity.

For myself, I like to say "I Love My Life," every morning as my feet hit the floor. As I do this, I am immediately changing my thoughts towards positive thoughts, because saying "I love my life" is a positive thought. Even when I don't feel like saying it, because maybe I'm too tired or I woke up from a bad dream, or I want to see the sun, not the rain, or I know I have a lot to do today, I still say it. Saying this positive thought as I get out of bed makes me turn my thoughts to the question: Do I Love My Life Today? When I feel myself thinking on the negative side, I turn it around and start to dwell on things to be thankful for. Positive and negative do not go hand in hand, so thinking that I love my life and saying things out loud that I am thankful for begin to turn my day around to positive intentions. I do truly love my life!

Statements like: I am making the best choices for my life today. I am learning to change my subconscious mind. I am renewing my mind. I am intending to walk this afternoon. I am worthy of love. I am loving myself. You get the drift...all these intentions start to help you change your outlook for today.

Again, being intentional is something that is done on purpose, or purposefully. It is deliberate, done consciously and calculated.

"It means you are purposeful in word and action. It means you live a life that is meaningful and fulfilling to you. It means you make thoughtful choices in your life. Being intentional means you actively interact and engage with your life."

Having said this, there might be great value in getting a pen and a piece of paper immediately and jotting down a list of things that you are intentional about or that you would like to be intentional about. While writing out your list, remember that the word "intent" is a "verb." A verb is a word used to describe action. So thinking about action, what can you jot down to describe intentional action?

MAXIMIZE YOUR POTENTIAL

To be intentional will help you maximize your potential in a huge way. Having purpose and a plan means that you have a starting point. This is fantastic. Without a plan, you probably won't get anywhere. When you set out a map of where you want to go, you then have guidelines on how to get there. It is the same way in other areas of your life. If you want to work on self improvement, then you will want to set some goals on how you are going to improve yourself. You will want some tools to help you in your journey. You may get some books on self-improvement, or a computer to watch self-help videos, or a mentor who can help you. Without a set goal, you might find valuable information, but you need a plan to put it into action. Being intentional, stating what you will do, makes it real in your mind and will move you to action.

Here is an example about going on a vacation. When you want to go on a holiday, you generally make a plan of where you want to go. You first decide on where you want to go. Then you decide if you want to fly or drive there.

If you decided you were going to drive, you would want to know what highway you should take to get there. You would not want to get in your vehicle and just drive around your city. You would need a map or directions to get you to your destination.

If you decided to fly, you would want to make reservations with the airline company. You wouldn't just show up at the airport expecting to get on the plane.

You need a plan or a purpose, you want to be intentional about your vacation or you will be highly disappointed in your holiday. A daily intention will set you up for success. When you intend to, you take action and you do it.

- I intend to read a chapter in my self help book today.
- I will state my affirmations daily to build my self confidence.
- I intend to go to the gym three times this week.

In the same way, stating your intentions daily will help you maximize your potential in other areas of your life.

CHAPTER 6 INTROSPECTION

INTROSPECTION

Have you ever practiced affirmations? Write down several that you think would help you.

_____

_____

_____

_____

_____

Now read them out loud. How did it sound to you?

_____

_____

_____

Try reading it out loud to yourself, but this time, pretend that you're announcing it to the world - the forcefulness in your voice should convince the imaginary crowd around you of what you just stated.

Now how did it sound? I hope that it sounded more forceful and convincing.

Keep repeating this until one of two things happens. You believe what you're saying is true, or that you are doing it automatically on "repeat" and not thinking about it. If the latter is true, it's time to take a break and try again later or tomorrow which is completely okay. Most people don't believe it the first time.

However, a lot of successful people have said that using affirmations daily in front of the mirror, can, and will, help you achieve your goals.

Check in with yourself every week to see how it's going with your affirmations. Do you believe them more than when you first started? What changes have they brought about? Are you more successful now than when you first started?

_____

_____

_____

_____

_____

Start thinking about your goals with relation to your affirmations. Just remember, your goals need to be SMART.

Specific
Measurable
Attainable
Realistic
Time Sensitive

Your goals need to be specific, not generic. For example, "I want to make more money," or "I want to help more people" does not work. "I want to increase my revenue by 10%" is better, but "I want to give 150 meals to people this quarter" is a very specific goal that even Tony Robbins would appreciate.

Your goal needs to be measurable. This is something you can track and not necessarily a number (though it often is). This way, you know when you hit your goal and if you didn't, you can see by how close you came.

The goal needs to be attainable. This means that it needs to be reasonable to reach. Don't set something too easy because it won't push you as much as a more challenging goal would. However, if you really struggle with goal setting and need to gain some momentum, it might be better to start with something more simple. When you think through what you want to achieve, make sure the goal pushes you out of your comfort zone, but is still reachable. Make it attainable.

Think of when you were a kid trying to reach the cookie jar on the top shelf just out of reach from the end of your fingertips. You found ways to stretch yourself out just a little bit more to pull what you wanted into your grasp. And finally after all that stretching, it sure felt good to get that cookie into your hand and fulfill your desire.

* * *

Our intention creates our reality.
-Wayne Dyer

CHAPTER SEVEN

KEEP A MORNING ROUTINE

Lingering on your favourite morning aroma.

I LOOK FORWARD to my coffee routine first thing every morning. I enjoy the sound of the coffee beans grinding to the right consistency in my grinder. I absolutely love the aroma of my freshly ground beans and I linger for just a moment on its scent. I listen intently for the "Tst Tst" from the steam wand as I steam my milk and create a rich froth. I watch as the espresso flows out and creates a smooth crema forming on top of the brew. I then pour the hot liquid into my favourite mug and admire my creation, the richness of the beans, its colour, and the velvety foam placed on top. Ahhh, I truly am a coffee lover.

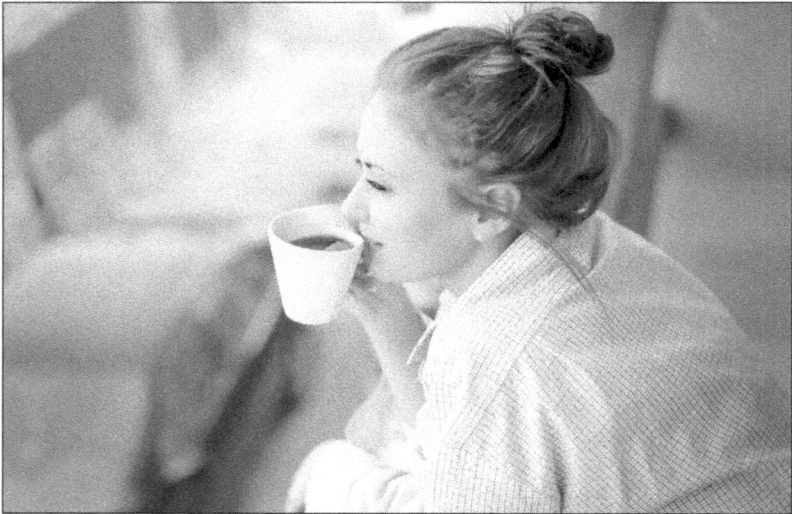

What is your favourite morning aroma? Do you have one? If not, may I suggest you indulge yourself into finding one. It can be coffee, like mine, or it might be a cool fresh scent, like freshly squeezed orange juice. It might be an essential oil or two - there are plenty of amazing oils to inhale - so start your day by opening up your favourite scent and breathing in its rich intoxicating aroma every morning. You might be surprised what these aromas will do for you and how they will help change your mood or alter your senses and turn your day into a positive one.

Along with this intentional positive action, following a routine seems to help many people and you might also benefit from a morning routine. A morning routine sets the tone for the whole day, and if you do each day right, you'll do life right.

Why do you suppose that is? Well I suppose to you that unless you have a morning routine, you might have the propensity to sleep in as late as possible, not giving yourself enough time to enjoy a coffee or read the newspaper, or scroll through Facebook, or have the time to envision your day or to do whatever it is you like to do first thing in the morning, and before you know it you will be skipping breakfast, speeding to work, creating a sense of panic that is totally unnecessary and certainly not good for your health and well-being.

Creating a routine for yourself allows you to make less decisions first thing in the morning and allows your creativity to be used elsewhere during the day. If picking out your clothes is a hard decision or one that causes you anxiety, then decide what you will wear to work before you go to bed the night before. If you are someone who needs to eat a substantial breakfast, prepare what you can the evening before. If you are someone who takes a bagged lunch to work, you can help yourself out by organizing your lunch the night before as well, or maybe even prepare lunches in advance on your days off, so you just have to grab and go from your own freezer. These small changes can be life savers and make your morning routine manageable.

John C. Maxwell says: "You will never change your life until you change something you do daily. The secret of your success is found in your daily routine."

MAXIMIZE YOUR POTENTIAL

By creating a morning routine, you will maximize your potential because you will waste less time. You know when you go to bed what you will do the following morning, and then you don't have to waste time wondering what you will do, when you will do it, or how you will do it.

Here is an example of how I boosted my potential with a morning routine. When I was in the midst of writing my book, I made a schedule that fit into my everyday work life. I knew if I wanted to get my book finished in a reasonable amount of time, the more I followed my morning routine, the sooner I would be holding my finished product. I made my morning routine a priority and it did maximize my potential. It worked!! Within 4 months, I held my completed book in my hands.

I set my alarm for 5am every morning. I would get up, make my coffee, get right down to business sitting down at my computer, and work on writing my book until 7am. Then I would get in the shower and get ready for work, and leave the house by 8am to be at work for 8:30am.

I owned my own business so I usually worked until 6pm, then came home, made dinner, and by 8pm I was back on my computer until 10pm. Then I had an hour or so of down time, until my alarm went off the next morning again.

I know this is a bit zealous, but I had a goal in mind, and I burned the midnight oil, as the saying goes, and got the job done. I used this skill of a morning routine to maximize my potential in this project and it worked for me, like it will work for you.

Whether you own your own business, are an employee or a manager, a morning routine can work to your advantage and help you maximize your potential and achieve your success.

CHAPTER 7 INTROSPECTION

INTROSPECTION

What is your current routine? Write it out. Start a vertical list of everything that you do and then assign times to it. How does your current routine feel? Is it rushed?

_____

_____

_____

_____

_____

Think about how you could maximize the efficiency of it or move things around to make it flow easier. This might allow you to be less rushed, and therefore less stressed. If things cannot be rearranged, consider waking up a little bit earlier to allow yourself a moment to catch your breath before taking off into the world. Does it look different?

_____

_____

_____

_____

_____

Have you experienced times in your life when your routine has been disrupted or times when there wasn't any routine? How well would you say that you functioned? Was it less effective? Why was there an absence of routine?

_____

_____

_____

_____

_____

Write down what your ideal, daily and morning routine look like? How far is that from where you are at now? Is this routine something you can start right away?

_____

_____

_____

_____

_____

* * *

The secret of your future is hidden in your daily routine.
-Mike Murdock

CHAPTER EIGHT

SMILE IN THE MIRROR

Smiling at yourself makes you smile inwardly as well.

STUDIES HAVE SHOWN THAT SMILING, forced or not, can have a positive effect on your mood, decrease stress levels, and even make everyone around you feel better.

With that in mind, why are you not smiling a lot more? A smile goes a long way. I know from signs related to "free smiles" in the Fast Food Industry that smiles are supposed to be a way of creating a perception of better service. I'm sure you would rather have a smile from someone serving you than a grouchy cold stare, no matter where you are.

Smiling is universal, but a smile can have different meanings. A smile can lift you up and brighten your day. If a coworker smiles at you after you have just finished a presentation, you feel good about yourself, taking that smile as a compliment that you have done a good job! When a doctor smiles at you, you feel a sense of comfort and maybe even relief about a situation. You generally have more faith and trust in a person that smiles at you than the one who has a blank stare, or a scowl. I would rather invest my money with a financial advisor who smiles at me and puts me at ease than one who gives me a cold, neutral face.

A smile is such a positive friendly response that can turn your day around in a flash. You in turn can make someone else's day in the same way by smiling at them. It can lift your spirits and make you feel better about yourself.

Here are 9 reasons why you should smile and a takeaway at the end.

1. Smiling is contagious.
2. Smiling lowers stress and anxiety.
3. Smiling releases endorphins.
4. You will be more attractive.
5. Smiling strengthens your immune system.
6. You will be more approachable.
7. Smiling will make you more comfortable.
8. You will seem more trustworthy.
9. You will be a better leader.

THE TAKEAWAY

Smiling is an easy way to boost your mood, be healthier, feel better, and be viewed as more trustworthy and a better leader. Whenever you're in a stressful situation or are feeling down, slap a grin on your face so you can take advantage of the many benefits smiling has to offer.

When was the last time you smiled inwardly?

It would seem that with so many benefits to smiling, you should be practicing smiling at yourself in the mirror. Turn that frown upside down and begin a habit of lifting yourself up before you head out the door. You might just be able to boost someone else's day without too much effort. Begin smiling in the mirror each time you brush your teeth and make a mental note at how it affects you each day in a more positive way.

MAXIMIZE YOUR POTENTIAL

How does smiling help to maximize your potential? Smiling, like stated earlier, makes people feel at ease.

Smiling would, therefore, definitely maximize your potential. If you were a financial investor and were looking for clients, having your clients trust you and feel safe with you is of utmost importance. It is doubtful that they would sign over their money to you without a trustworthy smile and a feeling of ease.

If you are in the service industry, a smile also goes a long way. You want return customers and you want their compliments to enhance your business. A smile might be the key that causes them to return to your place of business. In many other employment opportunities, a smile also goes a long way. If you are a hairdresser, or a server in a restaurant, a smile greatly benefits you when the customer pays the bill. The tipping point changes depending on the smile.

Smiling is one of the first things you notice when meeting a new person, or even a close friend. First impressions will always be a part of interaction, of who we are, and since smiling makes for a better first impression, it is something you will want to practice. Take time to smile today.

CHAPTER 8 INTROSPECTION

INTROSPECTION

Stand in front of the mirror and smile at yourself. Pay attention to the details in your face. Notice when you are smiling just as an attempt at it, versus when your smile is genuine.

Now think about something funny that has happened to you or a funny joke that makes you smile. Notice the genuineness of the smile. How does it make you feel?

_____

_____

_____

Now try this out in public. When you're walking down a side-walk or on a trail, smile at the people passing by you and say a warm "Hello" as you pass them. Do some of them say "hello" back or smile back?

_____

Do this in your normal day to day interactions. If you're ordering a coffee, as you walk up to the cash register, pause and give a big smile and see what kind of reaction you get. The more positive vibes you give out to the people around you, the more positive vibes you are going to receive.

* * *

Smile in the mirror. Do that every morning and you'll start to see a big difference in your life.

-Yoko Ono

CHAPTER NINE

DRESSING FOR OPPORTUNITY

Feeling good about the way you look makes you seem more confident.

YOU MAY BE SHAKING on the inside, but you look calm, cool and collected on the outside when you present yourself well. Do yourself a favour by getting dressed and ready for the day whether you work from home or outside of the home. Taking a shower makes you feel renewed and fresh. Doing your hair and makeup and/or shaving sets the tone for the way you feel and present yourself. You smile at yourself in the mirror and feel good about the way you look. Dress appropriately for what you have planned for the day. Are you in casual dress, business attire, a specific look you are wanting to achieve? Once you have made this decision, you are now ready for the opportunities that come your way today.

Opportunities are out there, but if you aren't prepared and ready for them, you could be missing out on a life changer.

Open up your mind and don't let the way you dress prevent you from any opportunity. Look your best, feel confident, and be ready for your day in a positive way.

Clinical psychologist Dr. Jennifer Baumgartner literally wrote the book on this phenomenon, which she calls the "psychology of dress." In "You Are What You Wear: What Your Clothes Reveal About You," she explains not only how psychology determines our clothing choices, but how to overcome key psychological issues your wardrobe might be bringing to light in your everyday life, or even at work.

Clothing can be an aid, good or bad, according to this article. I think clothing can help make your day either negative or positive, depending on what you choose to wear. You can get out of bed and stay in your pajamas all day, which I'm not saying is always bad because sometimes it's just what the doctor ordered, or pull on your old tattered comfy clothes and walk out into the world. What are you trying to achieve? You are looking for the positive, so let's focus on that aspect. Your clothes can definitely make a statement. For instance, wearing shorts when it's snowing out tells others that you are waiting for warmer weather and are trying to make a statement. You are "DONE" with winter! When you see people grocery shopping in their pajamas, you know they are just looking for comfort or maybe they just don't care how others perceive them.

According to an article by Peggy Drexler, Ph.D. a research psychologist, and Assistant Professor of Psychology at Weill Medical College, Cornell University, she says that clothes also dictate the role the people wearing them take on, whether we're talking about an upstanding man wearing a crisp button down shirt and good jeans to take a woman out for Sunday brunch or the no-good slouch showing up to take her to dinner in the sweats he's owned since college. A 1994 study out of North Illinois University found that people's perception of their own responsibility, competency, honesty, reliability, and trustworthiness, among other qualities, was heightened when they took a little more care in the clothing they put on.

Taking this into consideration, it makes sense that with all these positive heightened qualities or perception of oneself, you are sure to have a more positive productive day when dressing for success.

Do an experiment on yourself and follow up after a trial period to see if your days have improved and are more positive and productive than previously. Dress for success and become the person of your dreams.

MAXIMIZE YOUR POTENTIAL

Dressing for opportunity is a unique way to feel empowered throughout your day.

To maximize your potential means to be ready for any opportunity that comes your way. What opportunity are you looking for?

Are you looking for a business opportunity? Are you looking for a social opportunity? Are you looking for that *special* someone?

I had moved to a new city, was out of work and, even though I wasn't struggling financially yet, I knew I should be looking my best for any opportunity that would present itself to me.

Each morning before I headed out the door, I would get dressed as though I was going to my new place of work. Whether I went to a coffee shop, the bank, grocery shopping, or to an upscale restaurant, I dressed so that I would present myself ready for an interview. First impressions are lasting, and I wanted to meet people (with a smile) and have them think, "I wish she worked for me!" It is much better to be prepared for the opportunity than to have regrets about a missed opportunity that could have been prevented.

It wasn't too long (in this new city) before I met someone in a coffee shop, and because of a smile, we had a conversation. I was dressed for the opportunity; I felt confident in my interactions with this person, and this led me to a job.

This may not have happened to you, but you never know who you will meet, and who that person knows. Word of mouth goes a long way, especially when the first impression of dressing for success gave you the opportunity.

CHAPTER 9 INTROSPECTION

INTROSPECTION

Evaluate yourself right now. Do you take the time to dress the part for the person you want to be? This will be reflected in several ways. This is apparent from the choice of clothing you have to your personal grooming. Hygiene is also very important.

Have a look at the clothes that you have. Does your wardrobe need an overhaul? If you are at risk of being nominated for "What Not to Wear" then chances are you are not dressing for the right opportunities or opportunities are passing you by entirely.

What do you think your wardrobe looks like right now? Ask someone close to you what they think of how you dress for opportunities. What are their thoughts about it?

_____

_____

_____

_____

_____

Think about a time you were underdressed, whether it was a business function, or a wedding or some other event where you felt really underdressed. How did it make you feel?

Describe a time where you felt confident in how you were presenting yourself. How did you feel then?

_____

_____

_____

_____

_____

Think about the differences between both times of underdressed and confidently presentable. Think of the differences in how you felt each time. Do you think it was possible that those around you could sense how you felt? Do you think it was communicated in your own body language?

_____

_____

_____

_____

_____

* * *

It is important to dress for success.

-Russell Crowe

CHAPTER TEN

BEING THANKFUL

Putting it down on paper actually makes it real.

DO you ever stop and realize that it's time to let go of the negative talk in your life? We as a society have become so self-centered and focused on ourselves, we forget to embrace the good things and the free things in life we already have. We should be thankful for the beauty all around us, for the abundance of water, for the abundance of oxygen, for the abundance of trees and flowers. It is so easy to become lethargic and disparaging. It is so easy and comfortable to complain and to only see the negative things, and the things that need improving or that are wrong in the world around us.

You watch the News and you mostly see and hear things that are sad, tragedies or the destruction of humanity. Rarely do you hear about good stories with happy endings, or all the wonderful things that so many charities are doing for others, or even the positive things that the government carries out. The Media can affect your day quickly with fear and anxiety, so be observant of how this affects your mood and emotions. If you find that it brings you into a negative mindset, then consider switching channels or change it up and do something different.

I urge you to begin making a list of things to be thankful for. Add to your list daily, and read them over continually when your mind falls back to complaining.

Being thankful and ingraining your mind with gratitude renews your mind and makes you more positive. Here is a list of things to start with if you can't think of anything on your own. You might not be able to identify with all of them, because of where you are in your life right now, but pick the ones that work for you or think up some of your own.

1. I am thankful for sunshine to warm my body. (Some people can't be out in the sun)
2. I am thankful for rain to bring nourishment to the plants and trees. (Some people live in the desert)
3. I am thankful for wind to scatter the seeds for new growth. (Some people can't go outdoors to feel the wind)
4. I am thankful for snow and its picturesque beauty. (Some people live where they never see snow)
5. I am thankful for fresh air to breath and lungs that inhale and exhale deeply. (Some people are sick and can't breathe properly)
6. I am thankful for nature trails that renew my soul. (Some people can't get out in nature)
7. I am thankful for rest, even when sleep does not come. (Some people have no beds)
8. I am thankful for my home because I feel safe and comfortable in it. (Some people are homeless)
9. I am thankful for peace at this moment. (Some countries are at war)

10. I am thankful for freedom to worship in my country. (Some people don't have this freedom)
11. I am thankful for clarity of mind. (Some people suffer with brain damage)
12. I am thankful that I can get out of bed and look after myself. (Some people need full time care)
13. I am thankful for good healthy food. (Some people do not have enough food)
14. I am thankful for my family and their support. (Some people have no support)
15. I am thankful I can read. (Some people are illiterate)
16. I am thankful I can work and make an income. (Some people have disabilities that prevent them from working)
17. I am thankful my body can exercise, walk, run, workout etc. (Some people are too sick to exercise)
18. I am thankful for my neighbours. (Some people have no one to call on)
19. I am thankful for mountains and the majestic power they portray. (Some people do not have access to this beauty)
20. I am thankful for my good life. (Some people don't enjoy their lives and are in constant pain)

It is not always easy coming up with a list, and you certainly do not have to list 20 things at one time. Maybe you can only think of one thing right now and that's okay. It is still one positive thing for you to dwell on rather than none.

You may have different times in your life where you find it difficult to be thankful in your circumstances or your surroundings. Sometimes you are at a place in your life where you feel you have nothing to be thankful for. However, it is during these tough times that it is extra important to try and find something, one thing, that is a cause for a positive thought to dwell on. One grateful thought will renew your mind and being thankful will maximize your potential for this day.

Pressing on with an attitude of gratitude is a valuable tool that can stay with you for life and make each day a little more positive.

MAXIMIZE YOUR POTENTIAL

Being thankful will renew your mind and maximize your potential for whatever you set your mind to.

Some days it is difficult to be thankful. Here is how being thankful helped me maximize my potential.

When I was down and out because my husband was devastated with a debilitating illness, it was hard for me to be thankful. I wanted to wallow in my own misery, but I knew I needed to choose to be thankful. This was not an easy time.

I wanted to curl up and head back to bed, but that was not possible. I needed to choose to make the right decision, which was to give thanks for something, anything, and carry on with my day.

I mustered up the courage I needed, grabbed hold of my Bible, and relied on the strength from my God. I was thankful that

God was with me. I was thankful I still had my health. I was thankful I could go to work and earn an income. I was thankful for my family to support me. I could go on, but you see how I had to make a choice to go on and be thankful.

When I chose to be thankful, my day went much better, and my potential for earning was so much improved. I felt better about myself, and my resilience kicked in. Through my misfortune, I was able to maximize my potential and I realized I could help and support others going through similar situations. Through this dark valley in my life, an opportunity presented itself. I renewed my mind daily, and the journey helped me maximize my potential.

CHAPTER 10 INTROSPECTION

INTROSPECTION

It's also important to keep the frame of reference in mind as you contemplate thankfulness. The story of Tao: *The Watercourse Way*, by Alan Watts is a very good illustration of this.

> There was a farmer whose horse ran away. That evening the neighbors gathered to commiserate with him since this was such bad luck. He said, "May be." The next day the horse returned, but brought with it six wild horses, and the neighbors came exclaiming at his good fortune. He said, "May be." And then, the following day, his son tried to saddle and ride one of the wild horses, was thrown, and broke his leg.
>
> Again the neighbors came to offer their sympathy for the misfortune. He said, "May be." The day after that, conscription officers came to the village to seize young men for the army, but because of the broken leg the farmer's son was rejected. When the neighbors came in

to say how fortunately everything had turned out, he said, "May be."

Sometimes you can see when things happen for a good reason, and sometimes you aren't able to. Some things you can't understand, but if you believe that out of everything it is possible for something good to happen, then you have started to truly unlock your potential for success.

Start your own list of things that you are thankful for. Start with the big, meaningful aspects in your life and work your way down to the day-to-day routine.

_____

_____

_____

_____

_____

_____

_____

_____

_____

Journal your thoughts about thankfulness. Is there one more thing you can come up with to add to your list? Is it your spouse? Creator? Kids? Friends? Business partner? The roof over your head? Food to eat every day?

_____

_____

_____

_____

_____

Think about the people you know in your life that are like-minded. Who do you know that is thankful? Are you drawn to them? How do you feel when you spend time with them? Do they bring energy to your life?

_____

_____

_____

_____

_____

* * *

Gratitude makes sense of our past, brings peace for today, and creates a vision for tomorrow.

-Melody Beattie

CHAPTER ELEVEN

PAY IT FORWARD

Random acts of kindness bring fulfillment.

WHEN WAS the last time you were intentional about doing something kind for someone else without having any expectation in return? When was the last time you performed a random act of kindness? In your busy schedule and added busyness you place on yourself, you tend to forget that paying it forward, doing random acts of kindness actually gives you a sense of satisfaction and fulfillment that makes you come alive and feel more positive about yourself and those around you.

This intentional action can be very small, as insignificant as buying a coffee for the person behind you in the lineup, or bringing a loaf of bread to someone you know is under the weather, or shovelling the driveway for your neighbour, or helping someone across the street, or carrying out groceries for an elderly person.

There are many little random acts of kindness you can do that does not cost you anything, yet helps fulfill the inner part of you that craves the satisfaction of doing good for others. It lights up the receiving person's day, but probably does more for the giver ultimately with positive feelings for having done something "good" for humankind.

Random acts of kindness - Lend a helping hand. An old ancient book says it is better to give than to receive. Why, you ask? We all love receiving gifts, so why then is it better to give than to receive?

There are some health benefits to paying it forward according to an article I found.

"First of all, caring for others and doing things that benefit them more than yourself (random acts of kindness) has been shown to increase your brain's release of happy hormones, (endorphins) and regular release of these hormones is known to decrease stress, anxiety and depression. This can be referred to as "The Giver's Glow."

Another positive side effect of giving without strings attached, according to this article, is the body's release of oxytocin which expands your blood vessels and lowers blood pressure."

So paying it forward may be more beneficial to you than you realize. The added health benefits, along with the immediate pleasure or feel-good attitude it gives you is more than worth the effort. Paying it forward takes the focus off yourself which in turn may have a domino effect and, in general, will add positivity to your day.

Here are some excellent quotes regarding paying it forward.

"We make a living by what we get, but we make a life by what we give." - Winston Churchill

"The value of a man resides in what he gives and not in what he is capable of receiving." - Calvin Coolidge

"Make all you can, save all you can, give all you can." - Albert Einstein

Again, paying it forward doesn't necessarily have to be based on giving money or using money. Yes, that is certainly one way, but remember there are a number of other ways to pay it forward, so don't let lack of money prevent you from paying it forward.

Pay it forward and see how it comes back to you. It is the joy that keeps on giving.

MAXIMIZE YOUR POTENTIAL

How does paying it forward renew your mind and maximize your potential?

As the quotes above tell us, we make a life by what we give. The value of a man resides in what he gives. Give all you can.

Paying it forward will renew your spirit, bring value into your life, and will maximize your potential. If you look at the lives of great men and women that you respect and look up to, you will probably notice that they pay it forward in multiple ways.

The ancient book tells us that we reap what we sow. This means that the more we give, the more we will receive. Paying it forward will come back to you and you will be maximizing your potential.

Recently I was in a coffee shop and a soon-to-be-bride came in to order some drinks. I had the privilege of buying her drinks and adding some spontaneous fun to her day. I was able to tell her how beautiful she was, and that I was so excited for her to be getting married. I felt good about paying it forward and I'm sure she will remember the idea of paying it forward every year on her wedding day. Maybe I maximized her potential for a happier wedding day.

It may be said that maximizing your full potential truly does involve helping to maximize someone else's potential.

CHAPTER 11 INTROSPECTION

INTROSPECTION

Think of what an act of kindness is to you. Write down every act.

_____

_____

_____

_____

_____

Remember, they can be very simple and yet still very meaningful. Smiling at someone in the grocery store can be an act of kindness. Is there anything that you would add?

_____

_____

_____

_____

_____

Try to keep this task in the back of your mind throughout the day or even put a note on your mirror in the morning to think about what an act of kindness looks like. This is a great way to start your day.

Take that list and pick one item; try to do that act today for someone else. After you complete an act of kindness, take note of your current disposition. How did that make you feel?

_____

_____

_____

_____

_____

Put a mark beside the act so you can look back and see what you have done as the days go by. As you get more comfortable and better at this, try to pick ones that are more difficult for you. You will find that the more you do this, the less effort it takes and will eventually become subconscious and you won't even think about it.

You are reprogramming yourself to be more kind than you already are.

* * *

Kindness is the language which the deaf can hear and the blind can see.

-Mark Twain

AFTERWORD

I hope that you have enjoyed reading *Renew Your Mind, Maximize Your Potential*, and that you will try taking small steps each and every day to help make your day better. The little things you establish today can help you accomplish your bigger aspirations for tomorrow.

The thoughts in this book are from my heart. My desire is that you discover little things you can implement that will bring more positivity and more potential for success into your life. If even one of these tips has helped you in some small way, then I feel that this book has added value to your life. Many things in life take effort, and renewing your mind takes effort as well.

So to review, try changing one small thing in your life today that will help you renew your mind to maximize your potential. Enjoy the journey and help make the world a better place.

CHANGE YOUR THINKING, TRANSFORM YOUR LIFE

Envisioning a Positive Day.

The Importance of Daily Meditation.

Awakening in Nature.

Enjoy Daydreaming.

State Your Intention Daily.

Keep a Morning Routine.

Smile in the Mirror.

Dressing For Opportunity.

Being Thankful.

Pay it Forward.

REFERENCES

8 Ways Meditation Can Improve Your Life by Kristine Crane - https://www.huffingtonpost.com/2014/09/19/meditation-benefits_n_5842870.html

Mayo Clinic on walking benefits - https://www.mayoclinic.org/healthy-lifestyle/fitness/in-depth/walking/art-20046261

Taking A Walk In Nature Could Be The Best Thing You Do For Your Mood All Day - Carolyn Gregoire - The Huffington Post - https://www.huffingtonpost.com/2014/09/23/walk-nature-depression_n_5870134.html

Daydreaming list - http://www.bachelorsdegreeonline.com/blog/2012/the-scientifically-proven-benefits-of-daydreaming/

Being Intentional Meets Technology by Tanya Jones - Panoptic Foundations - https://panopticnews.com/foundations/being-intentional/

Be intentional in all you do! By Chrysta Bairre -

http://www.liveandlovework.com/2013/03/15/be-intentional-in-all-you-do/

Why Creating A Meaningful Morning Routine Will Make You More Successful by Cathryn Lavery - Huffingtonpost - https://www.huffingtonpost.com/cathryn-lavery/morning-routines_b_8042428.html

9 Surprising Reasons Why You Should Smile More by Alyssa Detweiler - https://inspiyr.com/9-benefits-of-smiling/

What Your Clothes Say About You by Clinical psychologist Dr. Jennifer Baumgartner - https://www.forbes.com/sites/learnvest/2012/04/03/what-your-clothes-say-about-you/#59ec3e616699

Why It Matters What We Wear by Peggy Drexler Ph.D. Psychology Today - https://www.psychologytoday.com/blog/our-gender-ourselves/201407/why-it-matters-what-we-wear

Health Benefits of Random Acts of Kindness by Chiro One Wellness Centers - https://www.chiroone.net/bewell/kindness

Ryff, Carol D. (1 January 1989). "Happiness is everything, or is it? Explorations on the meaning of psychological well-being.". *Journal of Personality and Social Psychology*. **57** (6): 1069–1081.

Help Guide. https://www.helpguide.org/articles/mental-health/building-better-mental-health.htm. Retrieved: July 2017.

Pictures from depositphotos.com

Quotes from www.brainyquote.com/quotes